The Diary of a Poetic Rose

By Anastasia Isabella

ISBN 978-1-257-87573-3

Copyright 2011 © All Rights Reserved

I dedicate, my book, to my loving mother, whose determination, strength and love has made me the woman I have become. Thank you mommy. I love you. Love Always Your Favorite Child..

Table of Contents

Page 3. The Diary of a Poetic Rose
Page 4. Who Can I Be?
Page 5. The Complete Opposite of Me
Page 6. Battered
Page 8. Hindrance
Page 9. Mistress
Page 10. She Survived it All
Page 11. The Beginning
Page 12. Not of this Mold
Page 13. Abyss
Page 14. Darkness
Page 15. Cosmic Universe
Page 16. Oppression
Page 17. Helpless
Page 18. Who I admire?
Page 19. A Rose's Revenge
Page 20. Ripped
Page 21. Rose's Revenge Part II
Page 22. Much Better
Page 23. Release
Page 24. The Keys To Success
Page 25. Free
Page 26. Tears
Page 27. Realize
Page 28. Maturity
Page 29. Friend of Me
Page 30. Envy
Page 31. Mirror Mirror
Page 32. Average
Page 33. Strong Minority
Page 34. The Personification of Strength
Page 35. Hold
Page 36. Love or Lust
Page 37. The Kiss
Page 38. My Perfect Man
Page 39. Treat Me Right Every Day
Page 40. I'm Speechless
Page 41. Goddes of Light
Page 42. Simply Poetic
Page 43. Soul
Page 44. State of Mind
Page 45. Anger
Page 46. Pathological Lies
Page 47. Looking Past You
Page 48. Potential of Time
Page 49. A Sister's Wish
Page 50. My Best Friend
Page 51. Darkness of Silence
Page 52. New Life
Page 53. Poetess of Reflection
Page 54. Exposed
Page 55. Beach
Page 56. Transcribe to My Heart
Page 57. Poetic Rose
Page 58. Poetic Stems
Page 59. Windows to my Soul
Page 60. Lips that Speak the Truth
Page 61. D.I.V.A.
Page 62. Poetic Fragrance
Page 63. Dreams

The Diary of a Poetic Rose

Open the pages of my world.
Enter my Poetic Diary,
Feel each emotion that boils up inside of me.

Find Me.

Reading the pages of my world,
I invite you to come learn,
My deep dark secrets,
My poetic endeavors,
Fears,
Passions,
Desires,
Aspirations,
And dreams,

These are the pages of my diary,
My words are whom I confide.
Feel my inner thoughts,
Immerse yourself in my words.
Embrace your cosmic energy,
Transcribe to my heart,
Reveal all the lies.

Where Poetry soars through the skies
It keeps my spirits high.
My words are my promise to myself to remain strong.

I uplift my mind with my words,
To understand my words is to understand my Soul.
Through the good the bad,
Through love lost and love found.
My words always keep me sound.

So enter my poetic world,
Watch me sprout from a bud to a delicate rose.
Turn the page to enter my world.
This is The Diary of a Poetic Rose..

~Anastasia~

"Who Can I Be?"

Destined for this life,
This cant be.
Constant struggle,
Always fighting,
Anger,
Screaming,
Disappointment,
Failure.
Trapped inside my own mind.
Some Days..
I feel as though I'm dying,
Emptiness,
Guilt,
Silence,
Depression,
Self Destruction.

Thoughts surround me,
Is this really all that life has to give?

Day by day,
Week by Week,
No relief in sight.

Despite the struggle I face,
I feel a faint flame in my heart,

I can see the struggles of life.
Is just Reality?
Am I just a number in this planet?
Or does my name have meaning?

Who can I be?

-Anastasia-

"The Complete Opposite of Me"

It is said opposites attract,

But is the Complete Opposite of Me,

Really what is best for me?

He has these traits
That captivate.

But still he is...

Self-assuming
Spiteful,
Lack of motivation,
Morally dead.

The Complete Opposite of Me

Rude,
Obnoxious,
Haughty,
Lack of loyalty.

The Complete Opposite of Me

Deceitful,
Sneaky,
Degrading,
Unreliable.

The Complete Opposite of Me

Yet he intrigues me.

His unfathomable ways,

The complete disregard for others.

The Complete Opposite of Me

I see good in his heart,
The little that exists and start making excuses.

Could his utter disregard of others,
Be just for display?

The Complete Opposite of Me

When he looks at me,
My heart melts.

Is it that bad boy attitude?
Hard Exterior,
Conceited personality,
Treatment like he is superior,
That attracts me?

The Complete Opposite of Me

Or that devilish grin,
That draws me in.

I think we are meant to be.
Or
Am I infatuated because he is..

The Complete Opposite of Me?

~Anastasia~

"Battered"

Battered and confused.
She stands there knowing she is abused,
As the blood drips down her face.

How much more can one woman take?
Before she seals her fate?
Is Death, what will come to her?
Or will she live in peril awaiting the final blow?

Confidence is what she needs,
To break the hold that he has of her.
No One deserves to be battered.

Whether its by words,
Or fists,
Or other abuse tactics.

It is Never OK to just sit back and take it.

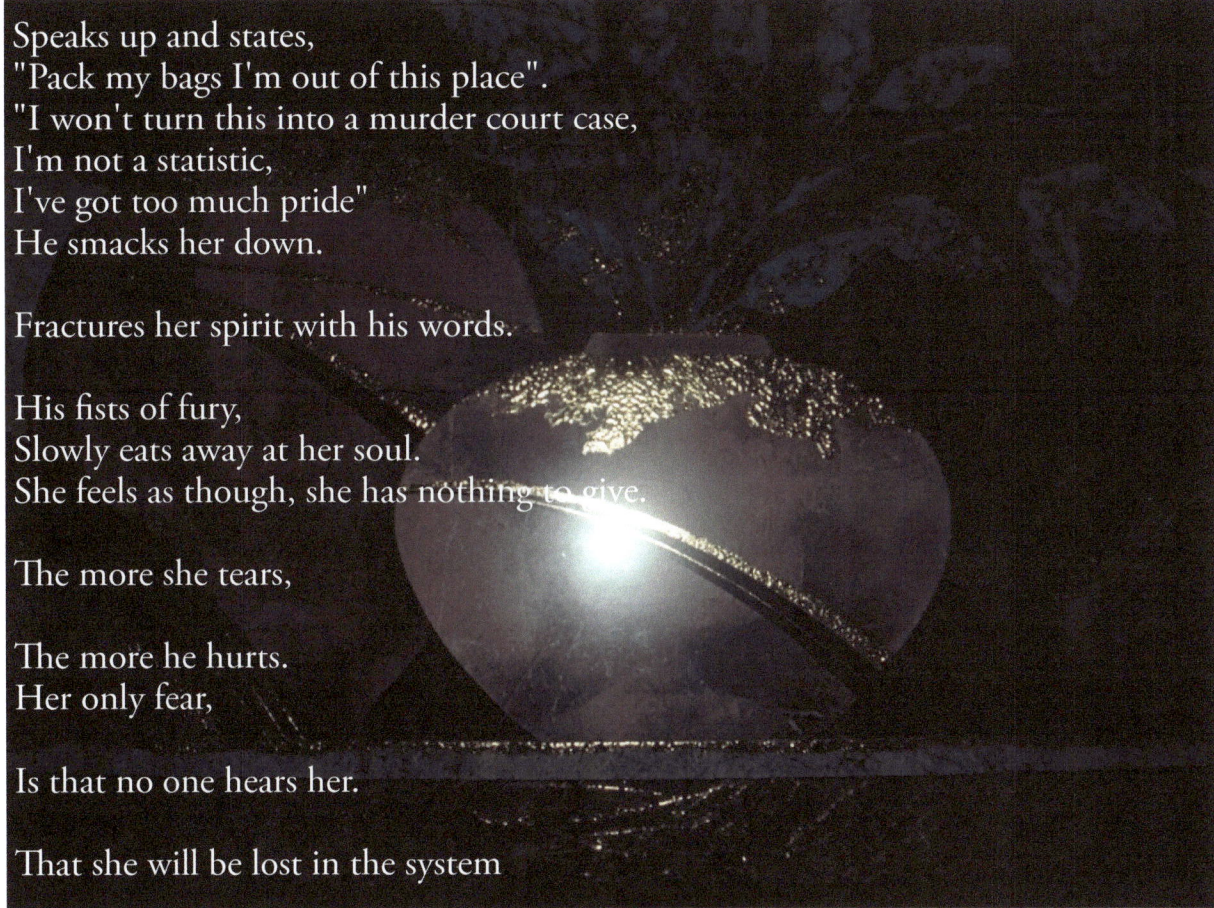

Speaks up and states,
"Pack my bags I'm out of this place".
"I won't turn this into a murder court case,
I'm not a statistic,
I've got too much pride"
He smacks her down.

Fractures her spirit with his words.

His fists of fury,
Slowly eats away at her soul.
She feels as though, she has nothing to give.

The more she tears,

The more he hurts.
Her only fear,

Is that no one hears her.

That she will be lost in the system

Forgotten

Has she embraced the abuse?
Does she now make excuses?

"He doesn't mean what he says,
I bumped my head on the bed".

Think back and ponder what you just said..
Face swollen,
Pride Bruised.

Does anyone care that she suffers this abuse?

All alone in this torture chamber.

This is her prison cell,

This I can tell.

She is staring in the mirror,

"Who is this woman looking back at me?"

She wonders?

Withered away to skin and bones,

Loss of strength,

But behind her glossy eyes,

She can sees a strong woman who is dying inside
She grabs her composure,
Wipes her blood soaked tears away.
Walks out the door,
Never to return.
She wont allow herself to be tortured anymore..

~Anastasia~

"Hindrance"

One Step forward,
Two Steps backwards.
Hindrance,
Is just a test of endurance.
Every objectivity and obstacle
Is a chance to prove,
The courage in which you possess.
Make changes,
Upgrade your life.
Better yourself and those who surround you.
Never allow your own self to hinder,
Any progress and fall straight to the ground.
Without knowledge people can cause you despair.
But be well prepared.
Continue to strive,
So you are not deprived.
Take each test and persevere,
Because without a hindrance,
We would never be able to attest our own fears.
Smile...
Without trials you can never grow.
So ask yourself...
Is this a hindrance?
Or just my opportunity for endurance?

~Anastasia~

"Mistress"

Its 2 o'clock in the morning,
The dawn is luring.
She awaits by the window,
Since her husband is not in her bed,
Lying next to her caressing her face,
As he should be.
She sees his headlights and veers out the window .
Before he pulls up in the driveway,
He quickly turns out the lights.
Being careful not to make a sound.
Because
He knows what will happen if she is awaken.
And that's not going down.
Creepin' to cheatin' in the night is what he is doing.
While she laid in bed,
Anticipating his return.
Her pulse was racing.
Each pounding of her heart beats more rapid,
As she hears him tip-toe up the stairs.
He thinks he has gotten away with it yet again.

Her crazy thought process.
She jumps back in bed,
To avoid an argument.
Pretends to sleep,
While he sits on their bed and kicks the shoes off his feet.

The scent of her perfume lingers the air,
Lipstick of his shirt collar.
Why didn't that man just shower?
She fights back the tears but the lingering stench of her cheap perfume,
Infects the air.
<Achoo>
She sneezes.
"Oh baby are you sick?", as he tries to take hold of her hand.

"No I'm not sick," she responds.
"I'm just allergic to your deceit and constant lies"
"You're so obvious, you don't even have the decency to try and hide".
You see all along she knew what he was doing.
Harnessed her strength to confront him,
of his cheating ways.
Envious

Developed a back bone.
"If a mistress is what you want you can have her.
Just don't come to my home anymore, (Looks him up and down) You do not belong ".
"You cheated with your body,
And put a hole in my heart".
Her husband stands up and stammers
"BBBut Baby baby, How can you be mad,
If it wasn't for cheating we wouldn't even be together. "

She stands there crying having all this regret,
Thinking back to how they met.
Late night walks
Dark restaurants,
Texts
Never any phone calls
Except the 3 in the morning, late night creep call.

Thinks to herself as she rubs her growing belly
Come to think of it,
I was his Mistress".
Now I'm stuck for the next 18 years ..
"Man back back is a ...."

~Anastasia~

"She Survived it All"

He did all he could to break her confidence.
Then went to Church on Sunday to fake a repentance.
He throws up his hands,
Clapping.
The music has him feeling emotion.
He is so full of himself,
I can't even fathom how he looks at himself in the mirror.
They look right past her.
She doesn't exist in his world.
She is just his wife and maid
Underpaid slave is what I would really like to say.
No one sees her pain.
As she sits there in the third row from the front,
He has to be seen put on a show.
So everyone knows his name.
She sits and thinks,
"This man is all for show".
The service ends and he smiles with a big grin on his face.
The whole congregation thinks the world of him.
Little do they know all the pain he gives in the "home"
Jumps in the car,
He turns to her,
Apologizes.
For the angry words he said.
Degrading her every chance he had.
Never once cared if it made her or the children sad.
No one saw her emotional scars.
He choked her with his words,
Every curse word you could imagine.
She lived in Fear.
And didn't even notice.
She had no idea she was abused by her husband.
That man she said those vows to in the sight of God and her friends.
'Till death do us part.
Until the end of time?

One day she looked over at her children,
Saw the pain in their eyes.
Finally realized.
That this house,
She slaved in day and night,
Was not a home.
She fought back she held her own.
No, she didn't hit back.
Pull out a gun or get into a shouting match.
She did it the corporate way.
She took him to Divorce Court.
And replayed,
All the years of mistreatment.
You see while others saw a
Shy
Frail
Subservient woman.
No one knew she had it all on tape.
Think about it and remember..

Those video cameras in the hallways,
Trips to the doctors,
She documented it all.
And ended up with
The house,
The car,
And the kids.
She Survived it All.

If you think you are fooling others just remember God knows who you are within.

~Anastasia~

"The Beginning"

A Rose's beginning,
I am beautiful, yet I don't know it.
I allow others to dictate my happiness,
Yet, I try not to show it.
I reflect on the day,
When I grew into a Rose,
It's a story so let me start from the beginning.
He told me he loved me to my face,
Then he insulted me every chance he got.
"You are too skinny,
your lips too big,
your eyes are too small
and fingers too long".
Yet all around me,
I stay oblivious to the emotional abuse,
and I hide.
He told the world I was a disgrace,
When he finally, Manned up, (so you can say)
He stuttered his words and this is what he said,
"Little girl,
So confused as to who you are,
Not sure of who you will become,
You are not good enough to be with me,
I don't love you.
Never have and probably never will."
"You are just cute, like a flower.
innocent,
Beautiful for a while,
Yet you wither and wilt
You have nothing to offer me,
And are unwilling to give me any.."
"This is how I see you,
So we cannot be together .
I have other endeavors
I require
Grown Women.
And you you are just a little flower.
so this breakup should have been a give in".

My heart sank to the floor,
How can the man I thought I loved
treat me so wrong?
" Oh go ahead start to cry,
that's all you are good for, too much emotions you have no back bone". is what he said.

"That's all I am to you after all we have been through?
I am reduced to not a girlfriend
Not even a human
A Flower?"

I boiled with rage.
Realizing that he was right I was
A flower.
I may start out as a bud,
But I develop when I am shown love.
My Style and shape are more than good they are great.
I'm sweet to the scent and my revenge...
Those are my thorns,
If he thinks he has gotten over on me..
I am A Rose and this is Only my Beginning.

~Anastasia~

"Not of this Mold"

Cold and alone?
Drowning in life's salacious woes.

Struggling to find ones place in this earth.
Without compromising on the only difference,

That makes up your sole existence.

Darkness.

Insignificance.
I am different.
I'm not of this mold.
Scared and afraid?

No, I'm smashing enemies pushing them aside.

I am full of rage.
Evil takes a back-seat.
As I spit out the competition.

Dispelling thoughts of my own demise
Never Compromise,
Who you are inside.
Awaken from the Darkness
Become your own ..
Never Be of this Mold.

~Anastasia~

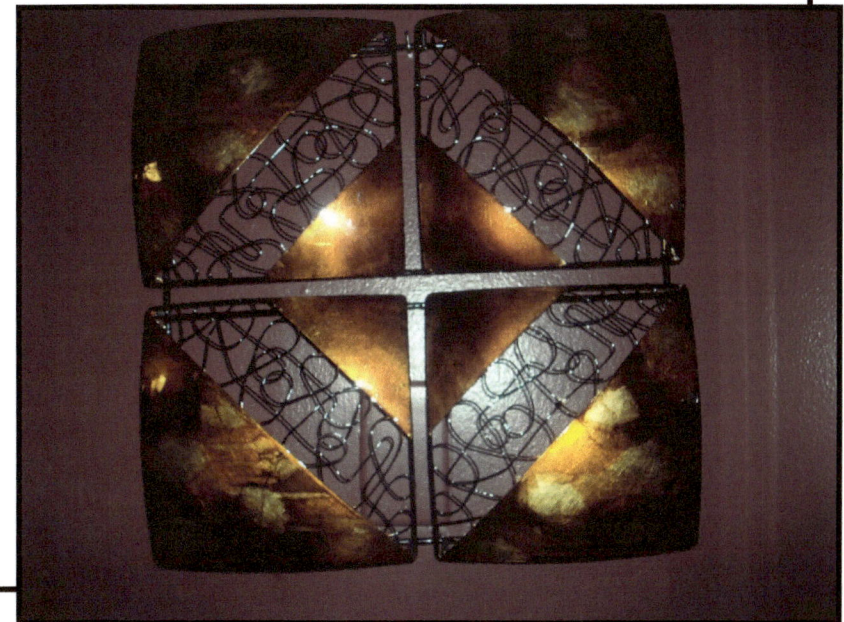

"Abyss"

Deep within the pits of my emotional abyss,
Where utter darkness is all around.
No light in sight.
Just the emotional bond that controls my soul.
Damaged.
Thrown about like the wind.
What was my heinous sin?

That I am stuck enduring through,
This infested wasteland of contentious hearts.
I'm trapped in this emotional bottomless abyss.
Where I am self destructing.
Assisting in my emotional suicide.
Crawling in the quick sand of my thoughts.
Where every move I make,
Keeps an unfathomable grip on my impatient nature.

I have to break free from the deep dark shadows
That temperament,
That molests my own psyche.
I cannot escape the facetious ways,
Where maintaining my sense of sanity
Is a vulgarity.
The blood curdling screams I hear.
Are my inner conscious breaking free.
I must break free from this abyss.
and come out of silence.
Even without confidence
I still possess common sense..

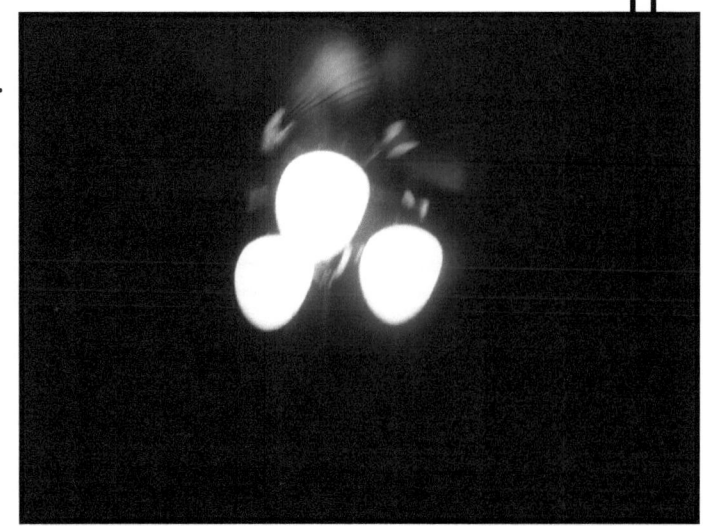

~Anastasia~

"Darkness"

Fortress of solitude,
Surrounded by the depths of darkness.
Looking for a glimmer of light,
To break the encrypting silence,
That suffocates,
My tenacious thought process.
Unwavering pain,
Without dark thoughts what would I gain?
Would I gain melodious harmony?
Inner peace?
Sanctuary?
Yet only for a moment?
My darkness makes me appreciate the light.
Enthrone myself to destined stature.
Without the darkness,
Would we appreciate the brightness?
A Queen is Me.
Darkness is my Light.

~Anastasia~

"Cosmic Universe"

Cosmic universe,
Thoughts transverse
Disposable words,
Once portrayed,
Now I'm slayed.
Cut down to the flesh,
Exposing the membranes of my inner workings.
Freedom is a term I have not known
Now I am learning and becoming as if we are one.

While staring high,
The incumbent expanse.
In this world we can feel so insignificant.
Free my soul now I'm letting,
Go...
As this world tries to consume me.
I break free from the restraints.
Now I am soaring high through the clouds.
Listening intently to the ,
Eclectic sounds,
Ringing in my ears.
In my world I have no fear.
Transform me and place me in this inner sanctum.
Free from the cold
Throw me into a black hole in outer space,
So complacency is what I can taste.
The epic starry night,
Not a cloud in sight.

Away from the madness.
Is where I find delight.
Without words,
We would be swallowed up by inconstancy.
An opaque movement.
To a translucent ending.
A cosmic universe is where I am ascending

~Anastasia~

"Oppression"

Trapped in a world of oppression.
Where skin color is a secret obsession.
Stomped down by people,

Who don't want to see a woman like me succeed?
Is it because of your greed?
Or Distaste for me?
The color of my skin?
Does it bring fear from within?

What is so scary about a woman blessed with a tan?
Are you afraid of what she can,
Put her mind to?

Do you fear me because I am an intelligent being?
Or is my brown skin all you are seeing?
Is it too much to bare?
That I have curly hair?
Were you raised to feel this way?
When I approach you do you fear the words to say?
Looking down upon me because I was blessed with hips.
And Luscious lips.

Do you look at me as a stereotype?
And get angered when I'm not about all the drama and hype?
Surprised that I didn't grow up in the ghetto?
Even more shocked to know my home is surrounded by meadows?
That I am educated and deserve the position I earned.
Despite the whispers that I was just an affirmative action suit.

Undeserved.
Know this I am not oppressed I earned all of this..
Like Martin Luther King says, "I will not use my fists"
I will use my diversity.
To help reveal the unempathetic thoughts of the shallow minded.
Still exists is this oppression.
Whether its a secret confession,
Or a slight deception.
Some ignorant people still wish we were still in oppression.
Where they rule as our bosses,
And we are thankful for our losses.

Break the Cycle.
Reveal the flaw in the mold.
Be **bold**.
When looked down upon for the color of your skin,
Smile and bring forth the strength from within.
I am blessed with a tan.
And a woman non the less with a position to do all that she can.

~Anastasia~

"Helpless"

I sit back in my solace of solitude.
Reflecting on the past.
The mistakes,
The transgressions,
The effortless ways,
To make me cry.
I'm sitting in the darkness,
Screaming for the light.
No one hears my blood curdling screams.
Because I scream in silence.
Silence you say,
The only outlet I have are the words I convey.
Helpless...
Destined to be alone.
Afraid to be undertaken.
I have to break free from the space.
Right now I'm stuck in this moment.
This time is now.
Where I'm struggling to find my true identity.
Helpless you say,
I have allowed myself to be beaten down by society.
And the caustic words portrayed.
Allowing myself to stay in this frame,
Now that's
Helpless,

~Anastasia~

"Who I admire?"

Who do you admire?
Answer my question who do you most admire?
I know who I admire.
A woman who inspires,
Fearless,
A woman who lives with no regrets.
Who illuminates through the darkness of this cold space.
A woman whose soul brightens the heart.

Ask me again who I admire?
That 5 ft 3 spit-fire.
Who mesmerizes by the curves of her hips.
Drives a man insane by the thought of her lips.
Brings a man to tears by her words.
Who I admire?
I admire the woman I am.
Through the good the bad,
There is no other.
If you don't admire the woman you are..
Then who will?

~Anastasia~

"A Rose's Revenge"

As beautiful and delicate,

As a Rose I am.

My thorns surround me to my very end.

You rip me out and cause me pain,

But in the end you get pricked,

By the thorns of my revenge.

~Anastasia~

"Ripped"

Ripped..
I just heard my heart split into pieces.
I am lost in my own thoughts.
Depressed isn't the word to explain my feelings.

I'm just torn.
Torn up about how it all ended.
Torn up about how I handled it.
Torn up about my actions.
Torn up about the guilt I have.
I am just ripped into pieces.
I'm lying on the floor,
Curled up in the fetal position.

Devastated.

I am weak
I didn't have the courage to speak.

Now what is important to me?
No longer being torn over the disappointments in life.

Nothing is perfect and sometimes,
Things are just not what they seem.

Acceptance
Is the key to find the beauty in me.
So I no longer see myself ripped into pieces
Can I accept the fact that I wasn't good enough?
But I am mended with needle and thread.
Patched up.
Filled with the love that I need for myself.

Silence.

I sit in silence to search for personal guidance.
No where to find it.
I keep my feelings locked inside.
I have nothing if I dont have love?

I am sad.
I Cry.
I love him.
I hate him.
I hate who I am.
Or do I hate him because I love him ?
Or am I am sad because I allowed myself to be ripped into pieces?

I am mad at myself bcause I didn't see through it
Now I am ripped to pieces.
I mend myself together with poetry
To make the pieces of me
A Brand New Me.

~Anastasia~

"Rose's Revenge Part II"

Roses are red,
Violets are blue.
You hurt me again,
I almost feel sorry for you.
For what the inevitable must do.
You may have did me harm,
By ripping me out,
But before I go,
Let me tell you what I am all about.
Look down and see,
Do you see a blood trail,
Limbs weakend like a slugglish snail.
I pricked you with the thorns of my revenge.
While you hurt me on the outside,
I poison you from within.
You are now infected,
With my poisonous venom.
Now I destroy you,
Slowly and painfully from the inside.
You thought you hurt me,
But it was only a bruise.
Cough cough
Spit up the infectious waste of your,
Seething personality.
Drip with your evil blood,
Knowing Im not your Mrs.
Cry because I'm not there by your side.
Mourn with pain because,
I'm no longer your lady.
And without me you go insane.
Rose petals,
My beautiful face.
Long stems,
My athletic legs
You called unsightly limbs.
Thorns of my revenge,
I may seem wilted and weak,
But my thorns protect me from being meek.
Tried to destroy me,
Burn me up in fire.
Yet I survived,
And stayed pretty until the end.
You thought I was unusable,
But with my thorns I'm unstoppable.
I was liberated,
No longer suffocated,
Once I left you.
Your life is ending,
While my journey is just beginning.
So thank you for bruising me,
because now I crush you with my success
A Rose's Revenge is now
A Business.
This is a story of "A Rose's Revenge Part II"

~Anastasia~

"Much Better"

In the darkness of my own abyss
No one care hear me scream
No one can save me from the hateful ways I feel
Deep ceded treachery
Is what is left of me
Nowhere to feel safe
No place to call home
Just these 4 walls that entrap me
Walls of
Negativity
Consternation
Trickery
And contentiousness
This is where you left me
Trapped in this cold damp place
Alone
Where is my home
This cant be my life
This is just my house
The holds my things
The Deception you left behind
Telling you I hate you doesn't give me
Peace of Mind
The only way to break free from this abyss
Is to kick down the door of your lies
Bust the windows of contention
With positivity
Knowing the truth that underlies
You need me to make yourself feel better
But I don't need you any longer
Because I am much better

~Anastasia~

"Release"

What you are is
Real arrogant
Your only Consistency
Is the condescending words you tell me
Never dependable on anything but negativity
Try to entrap me with those webs of lies
partially true apologies
Twisted into subtle insults
To break me down emotionally
I step back ….
To allow myself to breathe
Explore my inner conscious
And focus on my dreams
My future prospects
You see These dreams
My Dreams don't have room for idiocy
So allowing you in my life would be hypocrisy
So I must get up and leave
No don't try to stop me
This isn't a test
I am just too good for the likes of you
I watched my life disintegrate
Into a dark cold space
Where I couldn't even recognize myself in the mirror
I step back to reflect
To make everything clearer
Stare at this woman reflecting back at me in the mirror
Who do I see?
True innocence of me being clouded by the falsehood of your lies
Slowly dying inside
I'm choking on your arrogance
So that I cannot breathe
I cant stay with you
I just have to Let go
Live
And
Release

~Anastasia~

"The Keys To Success"

Motivation,

Determination,

Endurance,

Perseverance.

These are the keys to success.
Never allow Self-doubt, Deception, or Frustration
To fuel more aggravation.
While you may feel exasperated.
Downtrodden and alone.
Motivate and become energized by negativity.
Endure and Embrace each hardship,
Be determined to accomplish and exceedeach goal set before you.
Persevere through each trial.
And always remember there is no way you could have achieved anything without
The Keys to Success

~Anastasia~

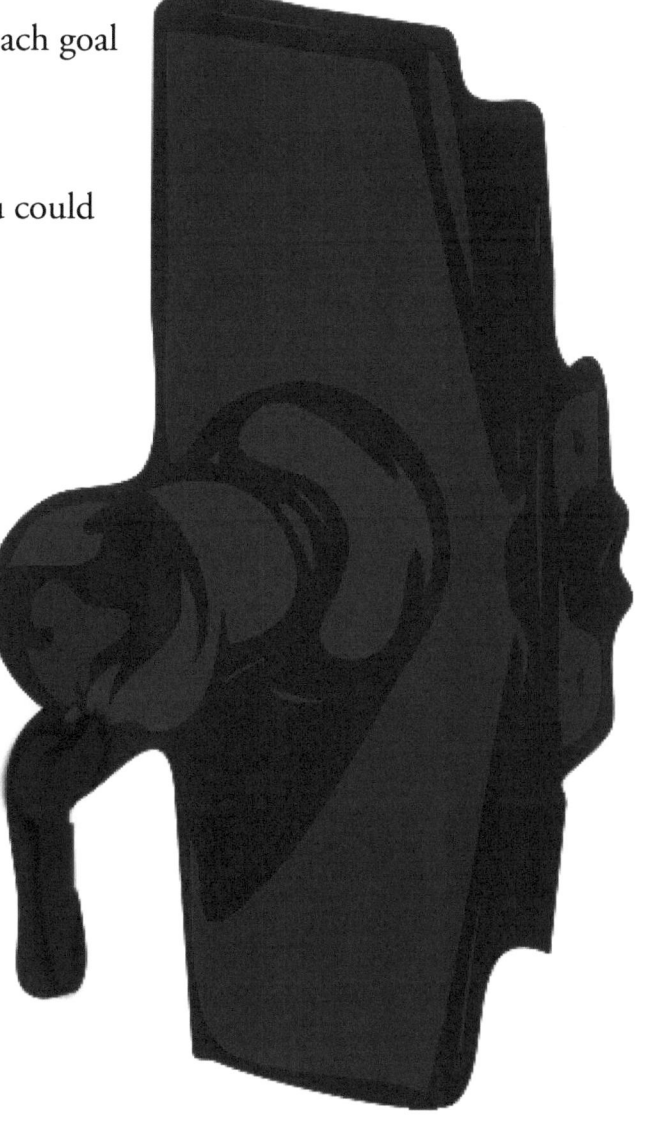

"Free"

Running away from the encrypting silence.
Embracing the vicarious thoughts of my own membrane.
Without my words, I could not maintain
My vibrancy,
Authenticity

I explore my mind,
Believing in myself.
Exploring the truth of my own psyche
I find my pride
Formerly terrified
I cannot allow myself to be restrained.
I pick my pride up
And nourish it back to health
With positive thoughts
I evolve myself to become someone to admire.
No Longer unbridled by the outside
Or restrained by the caustic mold,
That this world wants me to be.
Finding balance within myself,
I am free…
With this new found "freeness"
I strive to help change others
And find an inner peace worth more than wealth

~Anastasia~

"Tears"

Some days I sit and cry
Stemming from the emotional distress that plagues my inner self.
While others See tears as a sign of weakness
I know I emit confidence deep in the pits of my own self
The tears that drip down my face
slightly stinging my poetic face
It burns to feel the emotions i have inside.
Most days i do try to hide
Behind this outer facade
My tears cause no interference
They are just my outward expression
With each trickle down my cheek
I emit poetry
While my tears sting down my face
They free my body from the emotional waste
I shutter knowing I no longer hide my fears
Little do I know that each tear drop
Is the mending of my broken heart.
Bringing me to a new level.
Where emotions meet freedom,
And confidence replaces disgrace,
And tears are replaced with laughter...

While others may see my tears negatively
I see a woman growing up respectively
Each Tear I shed
is Poetry

~Anastasia~

"Realize"

Swallow your pride,
Drown in your own ignorance,
Finally Apologize..
Hope for forgiveness.
Give me a long awaited "I'm Sorry" for hurting me.
Cry out with eerie thoughts of dismay
Because I didn't allow myself to continue to be molded to your ways.
"Oh, I'm not who you thought I was supposed to be
Shy
Scared
Timid
And Lonely."
You See me now and live with Regret
Now your beset..
Dream of your perfect woman
You see your Vision
It's clear as day
I was your dream girl.
Now suffer and cry yourself to sleep.
Wish I stood beside,
To continue to be torn up and battered by your emotional abuse tactics
While I stand and smile to make you look good.
All the while…
I Grew into Confidence
Despite your complete disregard of my entire being.
Look who is now singing my admiration.
Is it you?
The little boy in grown man's clothes?
Who desires me back in his life?
I stand here A Woman who was wronged
Now I Glow with Pride
While you gravel at my feet,
Wishing you could take back the harsh cold ways of our so called relationship
Wishing…
How could you think you were so much better?
Do you see who you had?
A woman with some much talent she inspires someone everyday?
Now sit back and beat yourself up
For the wrong you have done in your life
You don't deserve my forgiveness
But I will give it…
And leave you with this..
"Read up on your own definition before you
Pass judgment and try to change others, You just may see a little boy not a man inside.." By the time you notice life
the motives have changed and it passes you by
You realize you have run out of time to rearrange
No time to change
no time to mourn
but time to accept and admit the mistakes of your past
Take chances
take risks
embark new paths.
So as each moment passes
And each second goes by take the time to realize what life you want and achieve your goals.
Don't let time waste
Don't look back and wonder where your time has gone
Motivate and use your time to make a life of your own

~Anastasia~

"Maturity"

Maturity...
Life is full of mistakes you make.
Without them how could we progress?
To grow to maturity?
The Good
The Bad
The Indifferent
The Erratic and Consistent
Are all stepping stones to reach your inner goal.
Once you have achieved this plateau,
Maturity
Helps you realize that the choices you made,
were not always the best ones
And yes, at times, you did not succeed but failed.
Loved the wrong person
Wished evil
plotted
schemed
with no real satisfaction inside.
Maturity
Without those mistakes,
bad decisions
or regrets
You would never reach true..
Maturity
These are today's life lessons,
The truth is what it seems.
Youth is wasted on the young.
We don't realize what we have until it is gone.
The Breath of life is a gift,
So use it.
Grow up,
Strive to Reach
Maturity

~Anastasia~

"Friend of Me"

Friend of Me,
Its hard to say who was really a friend to me
Growing up I had
Others try to make me feel guilty.

Took me for granted
Used me for my kindness.
I need personal guidance.
To break free from the mold of society.
Started to write and the words formed a hold with the emotions.
I was angry
I wanted to hurt all those people who thrived on my sadness.

Those who exasperated my kind nature,
Transformed me from a happy loving little girl bringing me to a dark place of solitude.
All hoping I remained Helpless in the game.

Taking me to a place of annoyance, anger and dismay.
Ended up getting burned by my desire.
I found solace in solitude.

I enjoyed exploring who I am.
I fell in love with Poetry
Grew into Confidence.
Educated my brain
And became
An Intelligent Self Sufficient Business woman .

So thanks to the former "friend of me
You helped me find True Friendship in Me

~Anastasia~

"Envy"

Envious you have nothing but hatred in your heart for me
Transpired to go against me
And still tricked yourself to call yourself a friend to me.
I am not fooled by selfish ways

I can distinctly see through the cloud of lies you try to hide behind.
A friend I am to your face
But you envy who I am.
You drip with green envy from your pores

Grow like mold spores
You are a infested in my life

I exterminate you with kindness
A friend you call me to my face
You deceive yourself into a place of guilt .

Staring in the mirror for you is an obstacle course
You cant look directly in your shameful eyes
All you can do is bop and weave
Try to achieve the best outcome ,
BY being envious of me.

Shocking that you feel I over looked our
heinous actions.
Trying to take my secrets and exploit them

While you remain greedy envious of me
I ignore you
Take a Second to Breathe
Exhale your negative greed.

I see through your outer shell of lies
I see the scared little girl you are inside..

Now you are completely exposed to me
Now who is going to go run and hide??

~Anastasia~

"Mirror Mirror"

Mirror Mirror on the wall,
Please show me the woman I am inside.
Show me a woman I know exists.
A woman of
Confidence
and Humility
Show me a woman with true abilities
Show me a woman who has learned from past experiences
A woman no longer afraid of her past
But someone who embraces each moment
Lives Learns and moves past it.
Mirror Mirror
What do I see?

Show me the silly little girl grown up
Show me her happy and full of love

Mirror Mirror
Make my vision clear
Show me a woman who loves herself
Who sees her past experiences
Dealt with them
And Moved passed.
Show me a woman who sees who she truly is inside
No longer timid or an illusive vision.

Show me the truth no longer distorted
She me Who I AM
Mirror Mirror
Please make my vision clearer

~Anastasia~

"Average"

Focused on the dreams that live inside.
Where my internal flame is fueled by negative atomic waves.
Little do they know that,
The harassment,
Bombardment,
Is only fuel to my fire.
So bring on the negativity,
Because its cold outside.
And with your hatred,
And distaste for me,
I don't need a jacket.
Because "I Got This".
Yet I stay warm by the fuel of my own desire.
Set a path,
Inspire.
Make a check list.
Because a woman of stature,
Is more than your average chick.
I immersed from the dark cold place,
Where I was hidden from society.
Tucked away in the dampen world that surrounds me.
Now I rise like the sun.
Glowing,
Emitting its rays.
Develop into a woman of
Forgiveness,
Style,
And Grace.

~Anastasia~

"Strong Minority"

Tired of being looked at as just a minority
When all around me I see the majority
Who I am?
A Woman of promise determination and drive
A Person in which others tend to strive
Individually sane to maintain my integrity
Without letting the ignorance of Vulgarity
Diminish my prominence.
In every sense,
This world teaches us to differentiate between Class, Wealth, Stature, Race and Color
Without my skin I would be no other
I wouldn't exist.
In this world full of indifference
The heartless majority are in bliss
Unaware of the effects in which discrimination has occurred
When you see me do you see my stature?
My Race ?
My Class,
My Color?
Take a look at yourself and see you for who you are
Not how people perceive you from afar
Love yourself because you are unique
Love every difference that makes you a minority
The way you speak, the clothes you wear,
The color of your skin, the texture of your hair
Realize you can change what you will become
But you can't change who you are

~Anastasia~

"The Personification of Strength"

My mind with each thought guides my way,
Orchestrating every action that I might take.
My heart thumps pumping my life force,
Echoing with strength
as my eyes peer with insight.
I am strong.
Capable of desire my lips form to speak the truth of my passion
My hips sway with my expression shaking from left to right
I am strong
Spellbound with the spirit of desire i endure through each pain
I am strong
With thighs that support my thunderous walk keeping me balanced in stature
I stay strong
Legs that have walked miles walking into happiness and turning my back from deception
I endure strength.
Strength and spirit blessed with the body from my ancestors
Strong by the size of my hips that mesmerize the heart of a man
Endurance seeps from my soul
As my feet though weary bangs the pavement with each stride
Strength I embody and I am clothed with pride
I am Strong
My body grows with strength while my mind enables me to do so.
I am the Personification of Strength

~Anastasia~

"Hold"

Hold me close,

Please protect me

The words I want to say

But my mouth stays shut.

My words can't escape.

Trapped in my brain

I am tormented sometimes by my own mind.

I want to scream and shout HELP ME"

But the words just wont come out.

I sit in silence and reflect on the turmoil.

Is this how my life is to be guided?

By the after effects of violence?

I can hear the disappointment.

The years of mistreatment

All I can do is write.

This is my therapy

Ease my pain

Avoid the awkward silence

The vivid memories that plague my inner psyche

Poetry is my escape from reality

~Anastasia~

"Love or Lust"

Covetous heart
Worlds apart
Burning desire
Alluring Touch
Thoughts transpire
As the sweat drips from my brow

Love or Lust
Companionship
Is this destiny?
Is this simply meant to be?
Fate?

Is this mere attraction?
Or am I drawn to him
Like a moth to a flame
I cant help but be near him

Even if it burns to the touch
That moment of bliss is worth it.

Is this love or hate...
Desire of the flesh
Temptress Eyes
Hearts Pounding
Love or Lust
Friendship
Devilish Smile
Love or Lust
Which one is it ?
I know what it is
Its is more than Lust
I care for his existence
It is more than love
More than affection
Its Poetry in a new Direction

~Anastasia~

"The Kiss"

Crimson ruby lips,

Awaits the first long awaited kiss.

As each moment passes,

Her breathe quickens.

Anticipation

Her throat is dry,

It is so intense she just might cry.

His Lips draw closer.

She stands there pondering this moment in disbelief.

Can this really be?

Her whole life is about to change,

And she doesn't even know it.

As she opens her mouth now moist with passion

Awaiting the seductive kiss.

She exhales the negativity,

Inhales the positive gift of poetry.

Presses her lips against his.

Intensity

Their hearts beat as one,

Continuous motion.

They no longer live separately,

But united as one.

He is poetry,

And Poetry is she.

~Anastasia~

"My Perfect Man"

His eyes are the telescopes to his soul
Staring in them warms my heart from the cold
The Grasp of his hand sends chills down my spine
I watch him in disbelief,
That he cannot be just mine.
Sensitive,
He is in Tune with My needs.
The smile on his face
Brightens my day
Strong Willed
Determined
Hardworking
Chiseled Man
Doing all he can
To make me feel like a Princess
No stories to confess
He is My work of Art
Laughs at my jokes,
And doesn't smoke.
Shares his emotions
Even rubs my legs with lotion
I Feel like he is a piece of heaven
Carved out of the sky
I want to spend all my time with him,
This I cannot lie
In my eyes he is the Perfect Man.
Feeling safe in his arms
He keeps me safe from harm
Believes in me .
Makes me feel like his partner.
When I walk in the room he sees no other.
He worries for me so I don't have to
Fixes my problems when I longer have the strength to.
Can say some things funny
Just to see a smile on my face.
Gives me deserved attention and knows when to give me space.
Throughout his day,
A Text message from him just to say,
Beautiful I am in every way.
So I feel special.
Without him I am just a Woman Incomplete
When we are together I am his Queen
And he is My King
He is my perfect Match
He is the Perfect Man for me
Is he Real or just a Fantasy?

~Anastasia~

"Treat Me Right Every Day"

Valentine's Day Rolls Its Head Every Year,
All around me, are the squeals and giggles
Woman who get all giddy with delight,
Anticipation of their future presents in sight.
Candy
Flowers
Or a cute fluffy stuffed teddy bear.
While I sit without a care,
People ask ," Why don't you care about Valentine's Day?
My Response, "I don't want a man who buys me gifts because its a holiday
I want to be put on a pedal-stool
Everyday"
Why because I deserve it.'
You see today is just a regular day for me
Because the man for me
Treats Me Right Everyday
A good man who understands my desires
Focused
A true gentleman
But don't get it twisted
Disrespect me and he is quick to defend
More than his girl I am his special lady
Celebrated and honored

Has no problem with me being a go getter
Pushes me to expand my talents and go bigger
This man
Is my biggest fan
Better than a lover and more than a friend
You see he
Treats Me Right Everyday
When I'm upset,
He does all he can to make me better
So Valentines Day
you can keep that
Because for me
I want a to be his hearts desire
His 5'3 spit fire
You see this man treats me right Everyday
and it cant get no better..

~Anastasia~

"I'm Speechless"

All my life I have had words to say,
Things that inspire me to write
A beautiful sunset
A child's laughter.
But.
Around you
<Sigh>
I'm Speechless
Finally get up the nerve to open my mouth
Form the words that I know in my heart I can speak.
<Gasps for air>
All I can do is search my brain to say "Hello"
Never before,
Did I think True Love could happen to me.
With you,
My icy cold veins
Melt away,
Leaving me
I'm Speechless
You and I
Are a perfect match
Perfect Balance

I give you my soul to keep,
My Heart is yours
Forever More
I'm Speechless
You entered my world
Completely understand
Take me by the hand,
I'm Speechless

Call me your Princess
Elevate me to Your Queen Sitting high on her throne
Adorne me with Affection
The finest set of jewelry He knows doesn't mean a thing tot me.
Its his attention
That makes me The Wealthiest Woman in the world
Tell me I'm worth it.

I'm Speechless

My heart pounds
At the sound of your voice
He gets on bended knee
And asks me, "Will you marry Me?"
Tears pour down my face.

I'm Speechless

He already knows what I want to say.
Kisses my Tears
As he says,
"In this world we live,
We are given a chance,
To give our heart to someone.
You gave your beautiful heart to me,
And for that ..

I'm Speechless

~Anastasia~

"Goddes of Light"

She stands there,
Glistening in the dawn,
As the illuminating rays
Highlight her beautiful skin tone.
Each beautiful feature more pronounce,
Her radiance is shown even more so in this light.
He stands there gazed in her beauty,
Spellbound by this vision,
An Earthly Goddess.
He tries to speak but,
Silence beseeches him.
As the sun begins to set,
She stands there as if she is glowing.
He is drawn to her inner energy,
And enticed by her outward beauty,
Awaiting the uprising of the ever- waving celestial moon.
The crisp summer breeze blows
Sweeping threw her hair..
Enchantment
He doesn't wish to speak to ruin this epic moment,
All he can do is stare.
The vision of her does more than capture his heart,
It tickles his spirit,
Awakens his soul,
Bringing him more than he ever thought was possible,
Warmth and peace.
Just in the comfort of her in sight.
He is drawn to her,
Like a Moth to a light.
He has to be near her even if it is just for tonight.
As he moves in closely her scent encapsulates him.
Taking him to a world so familiar.
Her sweet scent becomes clear.
This vision of beauty is not just a *Goddess of Light*
No, she is more than that
She is his loving Wife..

~Anastasia~

"Simply Poetic"

Embodied by the chains,

Holding back my thoughts I am restrained

Held back by others I can not contend

My Words are how I defend.

Hatred in my heart

Darkens my soul

Fear not,

What I am

For I am not of this eternal black hole.

Simplistic Words

Form audacious thoughts

I am what you are thinking

Am I not?

I cannot be conformed

I portray my own dignity.

I am most free

In solitude of my own thoughts,

Staring out the window

Envisioning my future,

My words Capture.

For one brief moment in time

My words express who I am inside.

I cannot change who I am

I am simply poetic

Love me or hate me

Either way I wont change,

Because I am Me

~Anastasia~

"Soul"

Reach into my heart,

Peer through my eyes,

Veer into the window of my dreams.

See how Poetry,

Is more than just words to me.

They are my outward expression,

Understanding my words

You hold the Key to *My Soul*

S pirit uplifted by the poetic words I form

O ften inspired by a distant storm

U nderlying exposure of unedited thoughts

L ove the fact that words can uplift a weary soul

~Anastasia~

"State of Mind"

Translucent prism
This world is my prison
Entrapped in the rage that fills it
Darkness
Acid rain the stings the depths of my soul
Brings forth ice
That flows through my veins
Cold- hearted to the outside
Warm to the touch
Thought I was terrorized by my past until i found poetry
With poetry I invite you inside
Explore the depths of my heart
Realize that in this world we are worlds apart
Deep entrusted hope is,
Turning the negative energy that surrounds me
Compressing it ever so tightly
To transform it into Positivity
Beaten down by the desperation that this world sounds
Weakened to the knees by the apprehension of the mind
I forcefully renounce the insidious ways
Transform failure into blossoming success
Each moment transitions
From self loathing
Condescension
To confidence
Arrogance
Into admiration
Success is a state of mind
Without focus and determination
Success cannot Exist
Just Think about it..

~Anastasia~

"Anger"

I battle with anger.
We go head to head.
Each day is a struggle,
A battle some might say.

I get angry at random things now.
Not just the thought of you,
The smell,
or hearing your name,
That makes me cringe.

It is everything and nothing that drives me to the point,
Where,

I'm hot to the touch as my blood begins to boil.
I want to take a torch and light my pain afire.
Kick down the tower of lies,
Dismantle the notion of finding the truth that lies beneath the terror of deceit.

Gnawing pain.

I want to gather my anger and focus it
Release the stench that lingers from the
Back stabbers,
Liars,
Deceivers
And all those in between.
To those who try to make my life menial and theirs supreme,

Expose them to the truth and see if they are immune to it.
Maybe the light will expose their lies.
Make them transparent so I can see through them.
I'm hot with anger and I know it

Let me try those breathing techniques.
Inhale
Exhale
and yet once again
NO its not working I'm still boiling with the anger that lies beneath my skin.

I'm so angry it starts to over flow from my brain and exposes from the top.
The only thing to keep me calm
Is the the sunlight
Breaking the dawn unveiling the light
I see my anger slowly dissipate.
Each day as the sun rises in my world I am given a second chance to control my anger
I write with anger in my heart
Let it flow from my veins
leaving them exposed on the paper
Oh anger..
I know I won this battle again.
My heart is at peace now.
So i can let my mind and body rest.
Some days, for me it just takes the breaking dawn of a new day to control my anger
At least for today
I won this battle...

~Anastasia~

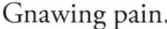

"Pathological Lies"

Pathological Lies.
You cannot help but give me these pathological lies.
Understatement of my intelligence like I am an after thought
A child you want to mold,
To be the under educated slave of a dominant master
Know who I am.
I am more than a Girl,
More than a Woman.
I am the internal Life force that makes your toes curl.
That after effects of a summer rain storm.
True Peace and Tranquility.
I see through the foggy seed of deception
Embrace the glimmer of light that shines through me
I hold onto your words as flaccid objects of your own demise
You cannot keep up with your pathological lies
If it wasn't for my drive
you could have over powered me
Battered me into oblivion
Beaten down
by the sadistic ways only you could portray
I made a mental note every time you lied
Saved them in the box of my heart
And exploited them when the chance arrived
I opened the box of deception
Exposing the truth that lies
It was hidden under lock and key
But since you insist on still Lying to me
You can keep your box of pathological lies
Because a woman like me
uses her xray vision to see
There is no truth in thee....

~Anastasia~

"Looking Past You"

You see you thought you had me
You thought you knew me

Little did you know
I wasn't looking at you
I was looking past you

So pick up your pride
Kick it to the curb

Because the woman of your dreams
Realized you are not what you seem

Kick down the door of disguise
Look at your self in the mirror

Realize

Your lies were real lies
And now I look past you with my real eyes
And my heart is now

Uncircumcised

By your arrogant nature
I'm over you and now I'm looking past you

~Anastasia~

"Potential of Time"

Dark cold night,
Twisted desires,
Fatal blows to the heart.
Fear of failure
Breaks the ever deafening silence.
As the poetic words,
Transcribe the thoughts of my mind.
Seeping out of my pores,
Unleashed from my poetic pen.
Beautiful moments can last a lifetime.
Words heighten each moment of time .
Dull moments in time,
Reality,
Now thought provoking instances of full potential.
Poetry of moments
The beauty of Time..

~Anastasia~

"A Sister's Wish"

Drowning in the thoughts of my sorrow.
I weep because you no longer have a tomorrow.
I mourn as each tear falls down my cheek.

What I would give to hear you speak.
One last time, one last hug.
Words can not express how much I miss you .
Today I mourn and hope I never forget you.

In my eyes you will always live on through the laughter of your son.
The smiles of your daughters.

Your spirit can rest easy knowing all of this.
I know if you were here you would give me those sweet hugs
Tell me I have nothing to fear,
To stop crying.
To Keep my head up and keep on trying.
I know you would be so proud of who I have become.

Tell me that the world still needs me here
Giving me one last wish from a sister
As I shed one more tear.

A Sister's Wish is one that can never part
You will always be in my heart.
My Last Wish is for you to know I will be okay.
and when we meet again one day...

I know you will look at me and smile and say,
You fulfilled my wish and I am so proud
Until we Meet again...

~Anastasia~

"My Best Friend"

Force a smile,
Clinch back the tears.
Stay Strong I remind myself,
Of her loving words that I hold close to my heart.

All the while I'm suffocating inside
Can't breathe
Try and hide
My stages of emotions
Come to terms,
that in this world we all are destined to die.

All I can do is grieve
Leave the words on the page
Try to help one person at a time
Help them grow strong
as she would want me to.

The pain I feel cuts so deep
Yet I can no longer weep
I am numb to these feelings
I no longer want to hear her name and burst into tears.

Yet I must admit my biggest fear,
Is that
I do my best to move passed and forget ..

No way can I ever forget my loving sister
My One True Sister.
I continue to pray for comfort

While I force myself to write my words
So my thought process can understand

She is no longer here as my biggest fan
But in the end,
When we meet again
I will bring a smile to her face.

Tell you all the craziness that went on in this place.
Tell you how your children are still my nieces and nephews

And how we moved on , Progressed to be grown up.
But still our hearts remained with you.

My words help me gain composure
Bring others into my world
Where you are no longer gone from my life
But my biggest support system by my side.

My Sister, today will never be a good day
For as long as I live..
But I will make sure your memory lives on

I wish you were here
To watch the take off of my blooming career
The birth of my children
Whom you would love so dear

But I give thanks,
That you are at peace
I just have to work harder
So I can see you again.
I miss you, my sister my heart , My Best Friend

~Anastasia~

"Darkness of Silence"

Deep Dark Secrets,
Chained to the sea of deception.
Silence.
Locked away in the darkness of the night.
Entrapped in the forbidden space.
Where can I hide?
Who holds the key?
To free me from my morbid mentality?
Is it you?
Or will it be me?
Who will unleash the words that terrorize me?
I keep my secrets tucked away,
Under lock and key.
No security breach,
Because my words are inside of me.
While others look in despair,
I embrace the darkness so deep,
Like the color of my black hair.
Darkness infects the air.
So I keep my secrets written with the stroke of my pen,
Darkness awakens me from the silence.

~Anastasia~

"New Life"

Words are merely flaccid,
Meaningless letters that,
When put together,
Can form a logical thought process.
But when you write from the heart,
You bring words to life.
Like an uprising sentiment.
Where negative thoughts are a give in
And happy moments are hidden
Far from the forefront
Soothe the trembling soul
Bring words from the mind
Blow into the nostrils
Breathe in ..
Give your words the gift of life.
Like the rhythmic beats of your favorite song
Hold closely the sound
Words are so profound.
They take on
Form
Shape
Color
But most importantly emotion.
Leave them bleeding on the page,
Drip
Drip
Drip
As each molecule of emotion is transcribed.
Transform lifeless letters
To long lasting
Poetic Works of Art
Words are needed
To Awaken My Poetic Mind
Bringing me to a new world
Poetry is a New Life

~Anastasia~

"Poetess of Reflection"

I had a dream last night,
one where I couldn't believe the sight.

I saw myself as a child
I was just 11 years old

i was sitting on my window sill
staring out at my cherry tree
writing words to form poetry.

This little girl is deep in thought,
Imagining where her life will lead.
I see her writing head tilted to the side
Her words are her outlet whom she confides.

I see the words she writes clear as day,
Her future thoughts
"The woman i have become.. is a Queen vibrant in every way .. a rose of freedom with confidence of a goddess yet still remains modest.."

Then She scribbles it out with her pen.
Lets out a loud sigh...
I'm not good at this.

This little girl so full of self doubt and anguish was me,
I see her cry and i know her pain inside.
She has no idea what talent she has,
How her words she writes will inspire others
How her story will make other stronger.

The little encouragement she receives
Is backhanded insults in the end
All you are good at is Numbers
Stick to that subject,
Writing will get you nowhere
is what she is told,

So she rips up her work and tosses them in the cold.
She is crying,
And doesn't realize her internal flame is burning inside,

I see all the potential in the world
in this little scared girl.
I cry out to myself..
Little girl, you will be a success one day,
Keep doing what you are doing and you will grow up to be me one day

The little girl looks over and stares at her bed
Where I am sitting like she heard every word I said.

Smiles and says,
"I will be successful one day,
Don't believe me Watch me."

This is the beginning of Anastasia Isabella
The Poetess of Reflection

~Anastasia~

"Exposed"

Strip away layers of deception.
Deceit suffocates me.
So I cannot breathe.
Removing the scent of resentment
Peel back the layer of skin
That oozes out of my pores,
The feeling inadequacy
Shed the tears of a deferred dream.
Seep into the depths
of who is the true me.
Vomit up the self doubt
Hear the outcry of a scorn woman inside
Spit out the lies
Which were used as a protection to hide.
Purge myself from the stench of defeat
Now I lie here naked and exposed.
Freedom is what I feel.
Floating away as though,
I'm flying in the air.
Bathe with honesty,
Clothe myself with inspiration.
Morph into sophistication
Embark on a new journey.
Lying in the midst
Being completely uninhibited,
Fully Exposed
Is the woman I want to be
staring back at me?

-Anastasia-

"Beach"

My words are like cascading tides
Deep within my ocean of life
I am never compromised
Poetry is my place of solitude
Like the crisp cool breeze that tickles my face
from the ocean air
Words..
Can Soothe the tempestuous soul
Transcribe the thoughts
Speak words unspoken
Perform life's song
Destined in this page of life.
Celestial Moon
Captive tides
Words are my best friend
whom I confide
This is my serenity
My words are my peace
This is my ocean of life
and Poetry is my Beach

~Anastasia~

"Transcribe to My Heart"

In the darkness,
You can hear the hollow screams
Of a turbulent queen.
She shouts in fear
Dreading the moments
Unsure if what she saw was real or just unclear
Save me from this intergalactic dream
Where love is backwards and nothing is what it seems
Torturous thoughts
Infect my membrane
Transcribe my heart
Etch them into the scroll of my life
Protect me from the thunderous rain storm
Where callous thoughts form
Though this storm is not all bad
It fuels my flame.
Rip through the pain
To find solace .
Scribe to my heart and poetry is what you will gain,
Can you save me from the thoughts of my own membrane?

~Anastasia~

"Poetic Rose"

Amidst the field of flowers
A Rose appears to stand alone
Different from the likes of others
Because her presence emits a radiance
She is surrounded by the warmth of the Sun
The beams of light shine down on her luxurious
Long stems
Showing each curvature of her fully grown leaves
Vibrant pop of color of her petals
Amazes your mind frame as ..
The fresh morning dew
Trickles from her thorns
Her protection from the mistreatment of others
Like tear drops they fall to the ground
no longer hidden
But reborn.
Into words of wisdom
Deep crimson red petals
Fall ever so gently
Blooming into exquisiteness
It feels as though it's a sin
To stare.
But you are drawn to her inner energy as you engage
in clamor you see her once blood soaked thorns
Thorns that can still cut deep if probed
Lustrous
With a feminine touch
Sensitive
Revenge is no longer needed
Forgiveness is a certain
As each petal basks in the warmth of the sun
She shimmers in the light
You cannot help but be attracted to her beauty
Drawing closer to get a full view in sight
You see the Beauty is not another but is Me
My words Uplift Me
Until I bloom
Into a Poetic Rose

~Anastasia~

"Poetic Stems"

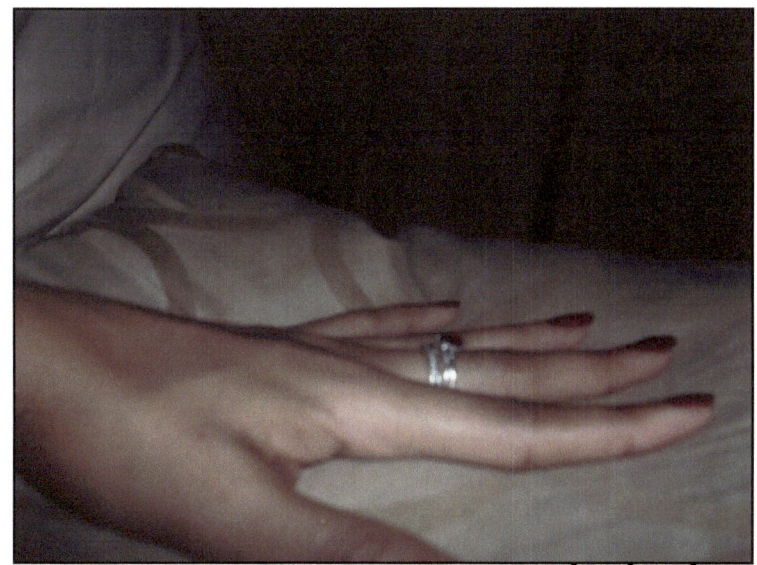

Hate me for my piano playing fingers,
Whose melodious touch still lingers.
Causing your mind to drift back,
And remember,
Sigh to yourself.
Wishing .....
Loving memories cloud your head.
My subtle stroke of genius,
As I massaged your temples,
Helping erase the troublesome days.
The gentle carassing of my long luxerious fingers
sifting thru each strand of your hair.
the warm embrace of my hand
makes you wish we were together
Lying peacfully basking in the sand.
How you wish those unsightly fingers you called them
Were grasping your hand.
Keeping you close
Im no longer a girl,
I am a woman
I embrace myself and love
what Im doing
So dream on and wish
Go ahead and remenise
Now Unfortunately my hands are allergic to you
They no longer need you
So while you sit back
reminese on the sweet touches from my fingers
Im waving good bye because you are out of my life
With my long Poetic Stems

~Anastasia~

"Windows to my Soul"

Deep brown eyes,
What I used to hate.
Wasn't good enough to be seen,
Hidden from society.
Was told they were too small, yet to wide...

I was embarrassed of my eyes.
Why?
These almond shaped visions of my spirit.
The focal point of my vision to achieve my dreams.
With my eyes I see everything clear.
Hated because they see through the cloud of taunting lies

Seeing the truth.
Piercing like a sword.
Mind boggling,
Glowing in the light.
My eyes not only make me who I am,
But scan through the evil patrons.

I see though phonies and habitual liars.
My eyes pierce through them
And expose.
To see me is to stare through my visions of purity
And find a moment of clarity
Formerly closed off from the world
I concealed my true beauty

I allowed myself to be controlled
Dictated and I faltered
Now with visions of loveliness
I open my eyes
Allow the floodgates of tears to arise
Eyes once hated
Now mesmerize
Hated only because deep down inside
 it was known that my eyes would expose the true essence
Of the unabridged deceptions
No longer blind to the obvious
 My eyes awaken
These are the windows to my being
The windows to my soul

~Anastasia~

"Lips that Speak the Truth"

Succulent Lips

Full of intense emotions

I wished my lips would just disappear

But hiding these luscious lips

Is hard to accomplish

Since its intensity is superseded by the unachievable

My mouth opens speaking the truth

Putting poetic thoughts to unequivocal poetic words

Spoken out loud

Yet so gentle to the touch

Like soft fluffy pillows

You just want to snuggle

What was once considered an imperfection

Clouded and distorted in my head

Now speak the words I so desperately wanted to say

Longing for its perfect match

To fill in the gap

Find that true love kiss

I Speak the truth no longer hidden by my luscious lips

~Anastasia~

"D.I.V.A."

A Diva.
What is a Diva?

I am a Diva, yes I am.
A Diva takes pride In appearance and emits confidence.

I love to dress up,
Heels,
Jewelry,
And accessories.
I love it all.

Some call me conceited,
But that's cool with me,
because a Diva like me,
Has the right amount of confidence and classiness to take the insults. Subtle comments spoken about me, to down grade my personality.
I conform it and make it a success. Yes, I am a Diva, and I love who I am.
But before you cast judgment read Up on the acronym.

A Diva since you show distaste for it let me describe it:

D stands for determination
I is for inspiration
V is for vivacious and
A is for aspiring ...

Put it all together and sweetie you got me.

I am a Diva.
An entrepreneur.

I took the negativity given to me flipped it positively and turned it into a business.

Now that's a true Diva.
So to answer the question, yes I admit it, a Diva is who I am.
And I not only love it.
I embrace it ..

Smooches...

~Anastasia~

"Poetic Fragrance"

The Scent of my Poetic Fragrance

My Poetic aroma brings a calming perfume in the air.
Where words form without a care
Carefully placed
To draw in a sweet smelling scent
A poetic atmosphere

Inhale my words,
Breathe in my sweet poetic fragrance
Exhale the stench of inferiority
And the filthy evil thoughts that try to creep up from behind.

Intoxicate your mind
Elevate your poetic senses,
Bring yourself to a new high.
No need for drugs or alcohol
Poetry reaches the soul

Join me on a poetic adventure.
Where we travel through the depths of our minds

Curl up to my aroma therapy
That seeps into your pores
Unleash the scent of poetry

I bathe myself in the scent of poetry
It soothes the mind and body.

Keeping the stench that permeates the disease encrusted world
Slowly poisoning me to feel unfurled

I write these words and form poetry
Making a new scent
It smells so good you can taste it.

Drift away into poetic elegance
Can you smell my Poetic fragrance?.

~Anastasia~

"Dreams"

I used to be a girl who was forced to have her dreams deferred.

I used to be a girl who was so full of animosity and anger

I used to be a girl who could not find my way

I am no longer a girl I am a woman

I have survived through trials

I have survived through scares

I have survived through heartbreaks and hardships

I am alive

I am thankful to my God above

I am living my Dream

no longer deferred

I am now my own Queen

Liars Deception facetiousness

deceit those traits and people are now of my past

I cannot change what has happened in the past

I can only grow and embrace the reality that is my life.

I am me and there is no denying that I have my faults

But at the end of the day I am a woman who is now staying true to my thoughts and beliefs

I am my own Queen

Because I no longer have dreams I am living my dream

~Anastasia~

Bio

My name is Anastasia Isabella. I came into this world on the 16th day of July. Growing up as the youngest child in my family, I was very shy, quiet and timid around others.

I began writing poetry at the age of 11 years old, as a way to organize my emotions.

Yet, I kept my poetry a secret, due to fear that it would not exceed expectations beset before me. So I kept a journal of my poetry and hide it under my bed for years.

When I finally started breaking out of my shy shell a the age of 16, I submitted a short haiku into an online poetry contest. When my poem won first prize, I knew that I had found my passion in life. Even if the language is not the same, the emotions of the poem can still be translated. Poetry uplifts my heart and breathes life into my soul.

In my spare time I enjoy cooking, trying various flavors of food, baking, dancing, and of course fashion. I love clothes, shoes, accessories and creating a new look with each piece. I feel that Poetry, Food and Fashion emit from my soul and make me a DIVA.

Determined
Inspirational
Vivacious
Aspiring entrepreneur

My motto is "Keep Sharing the Dream and Stay Inspired". This book is helping me achieve my Dream and keeping me Inspired.

~ Always Ana ~

Visit me at:
www.anapoeticrose.com